IMAGES OF ENGLAND

PLYMOUTH
AT WAR

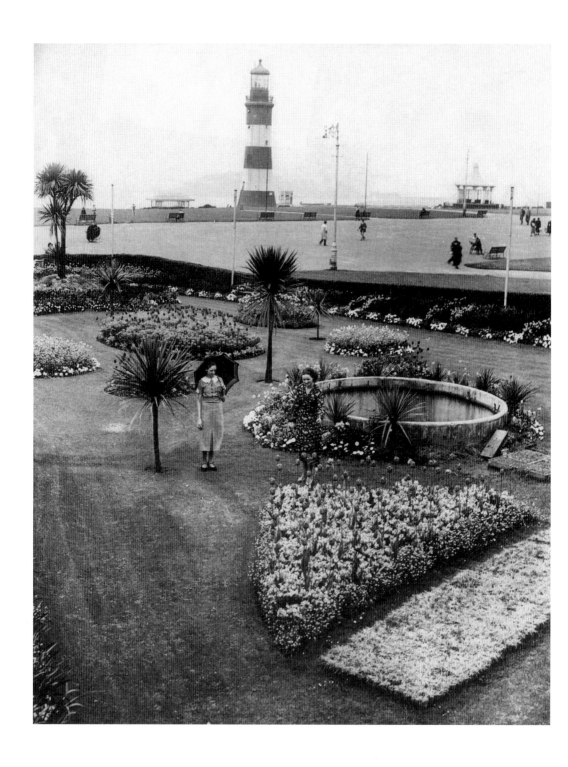

IMAGES OF ENGLAND

PLYMOUTH AT WAR

DEREK TAIT

TEMPUS

Frontispiece: A pre-war view of Plymouth Hoe. The bandstand which can been seen in the background was totally destroyed during the Blitz of 1941, when Plymouth sustained its heaviest bombing. Two girls in the foreground admire the tulips and, as this is Plymouth, one has an umbrella!

First published 2006

Tempus Publishing Limited
The Mill, Brimscombe Port,
Stroud, Gloucestershire, GL5 2QG
www.tempus-publishing.com

British Library Cataloguing in Publication Data.
A catalogue record for this book is available from the British Library.

ISBN 0 7524 3850 6

Typesetting and origination by Tempus Publishing Limited.
Printed in Great Britain.

Contents

Acknowledgements

Thanks to the *Western Morning News* for letting me use their archive photographs. Many of these were taken by their staff photographers, including Dermot Fitzgerald and Stanley Green.

Also thanks to Maurice Dart, Eric Webb, Steve Johnson, Jim Davis, Tina Cole, Ellen Tait, Alan Tait, Keith Parker, Sally Ware, Howard Beveridge and Sam Mitchell for other photographs that appear in the book.

I would also like to thank Guy Fleming, Frank Wintle, Brian Moseley and Roy Westlake for their help and advice.

I have done my best to track down the owners of the copyright of all images used and apologise to anyone not mentioned.

Bibliography

PUBLICATIONS

Mike Brown, *Put That Light Out!* (Sutton Publishing, 1999)
Arthur Clamp, *Blitz of Plymouth 1940-1944* (PDS Printers, 1981)
Andrew Cluer and Ron Winram, *Plymouth and Plymothians* (Winram-Cluer Publications, 1985)
R.F.E. Cock, *Plymouth Blitz* (publisher unknown, 1940s)
Jim Davis, *Winged Victory* (R.J. Leach and Co., 1995)
Guy Fleming, *Plymouth: Pictures from the Past* (Devon Books, 1994)
Guy Fleming, *Plymouth: More Pictures from the Past* (Devon Books, 1996)
Kevin Scrivener, *Plymouth at War* (Archive Publications, 1989)
H.P. Twyford, *It Came to Our Door* (1947)
H.P. Twyford, *Plymouth Blitz: The Story of the Raids* (*Western Morning News*, 1947)
Gerald Wasley, *Plymouth: A Shattered City* (Halsgrove, 2003)
Frank Wintle, *Plymouth Blitz* (Bossiney, 1985)

NEWSPAPERS

Western Morning News
Evening Herald

WEBSITES

Boots at www.boots-plc.com
Steve Johnson's Cyberheritage at www.cyberheritage.co.uk
Brian Moseley's Plymouth Data at www.plymouthdata.info
Chris Robinson at www.chrisrobinson.co.uk

Introduction

Plymouth would be a very different city today were it not for the Blitz of the Second World War. The city suffered perhaps the most damage during the devastation dealt out by the Luftwaffe in 1941. At the time, the American magazine *Life* reported in its pages that 'Plymouth is worse than it looks', and it looked pretty bad. London, Coventry and Bristol suffered severe damage during the war but all agreed that Plymouth was in the sorriest state, with much of the centre completely obliterated. Amazingly, Plymouth once thought itself to be so far away from military attacks and hostility that it would escape the heavy bombing. However, the dockyard was an ever-tempting prospect to the Germans, as were the railways and fuel depots.

It's hard to imagine the lively, bustling city of Plymouth before the bombs dropped because so much has now changed and been rebuilt. Plymouth in 1940 was a busy city with cars, buses and trams all running side by side. Shops, cafés and restaurants overflowed with customers. The first bombs fell on the city on 6 July 1940, when houses at Swilly Road were hit. There were several casualties. In later attacks, shelters in the city centre were crowded with shoppers and one store even served coffee as the bombs fell. Air-raid wardens would clear the streets of people who refused to take cover.

This was a time when the sound of an air-raid siren would have you rushing out of your house and into the garden to take cover in a purpose-built Anderson shelter. It was a time when food, clothing and other essentials were all rationed, and when you had to take a gas mask with you everywhere you went, for fear of an enemy attack. It is almost unimaginable today.

Civil defence forces were brought together and did a great job. These included firefighters, first-aiders and, of course, the Home Guard. The Home Guard wasn't a rag-tag bunch of men as featured in *Dad's Army* but were a well-trained force, ready to deal with any eventuality. Air-raid control centres were based underneath the Guildhall and also beneath Devonport market. They proved to be the nerve centres during attacks.

The heaviest attacks on the city came in 1941. In the two intensive attacks on 20 and 21 March, 336 people lost their lives. Five further attacks in April brought the toll to 590. There was hardly a building in Plymouth that wasn't touched in some way by the Blitz. Much of the city centre was obliterated and although many buildings remained among the debris, most were damaged beyond repair. It's hard now to comprehend the total destruction the bombing caused. Many of the main streets, including Bedford Street, Union Street, Old Town Street, Frankfort Street, Cornwall Street and George Street, were either totally destroyed or severely damaged. Major buildings such as the Guildhall, the Municipal Buildings, St Andrew's church, Charles church and the general post office were devastated.

Many schools were also hit. These included Plymouth High School for Girls, the Hoe Grammar School and the infants' school at Summerland Place. Many churches were destroyed, including St James the Less, King Street Methodist, St Peter's, George Street Baptist and many more. The bombing was indiscriminate and destroyed anything that got in its way.

In the dockyard the bombing was bad but not as damaging as was at first thought, and within a few months it was back to 90 per cent efficiency. Outside the city, the bombing was just as devastating and areas affected included Devonport, Stonehouse, St Budeaux, Swilly and Saltash Passage. Devonport lost many buildings, including the post office, the Alhambra Theatre, the synagogue, the Hippodrome and the Salvation Army headquarters.

Residential houses that were either destroyed or beyond repair amounted to 3,754. Others that were seriously damaged but able to be repaired amounted to 18,398. Houses that were slightly damaged amounted to an additional 49,950. It's hard to imagine such devastation to a city unless you've lived through it. At the end of the war, there were a total of 4,448 casualties due to the raids and heavy bombing of the city.

Many children were evacuated from the city to live with relatives, friends or obliging families in safe areas in the countryside. Thousands left on special trains and many saw it as an adventure while others were upset to leave their parents behind. Lady Astor said at the time, 'What helped the evacuation was that everyone seemed to have a cousin in the country!'

News of the devastation of Plymouth soon reached the rest of the world and gifts arrived from all over, particularly from the United States, who sent ambulances, soft toys, food packages and surgical dressings. The Royal Sailors' Rest received crates of supplies so large that they were unable to get them into the building.

Throughout it all, though, the people of Plymouth remained strong and there were regular dances on the Hoe almost in defiance of the enemy as they bombed the city. Plymouth was reborn after the war and the city was rebuilt almost from scratch. Few buildings that were there before the war remained in the heart of the city and, even now, the city is constantly changing. Here, in over 200 photographs, is a brief look at what the city and its people were once like.

Derek Tait
January 2006

one

Pre-war Plymouth

Bedford Street and Basket Street in the 1940s, before the Blitz. On the right can be seen Tucketts and in the centre of the picture is Bateman's opticians with their trademark pair of large spectacles. Bedford Street was a busy thoroughfare at the time and cars, trams and buses can all be seen running side by side.

St Andrew's church and the Guildhall, with its pleasant garden area, looking across the tramlines to Bedford Street. On 20 March 1941, the church was severely damaged but not thought to be beyond repair. However, on 21 March, the church was hit again, leaving only the walls and tower still standing.

Above: Uglow's café was a popular place for refreshments. It was situated in Lockyer Street, ideally placed for people on their way to or from the Hoe. The building had previously housed the YWCA. Lockyer Street also housed an ARP shelter and a first-aid post during the war. The Prince of Wales Hospital in Lockyer Street was bombed but was later reopened.

Right: Bedford Street. Timothy White's, a hardware, home and garden store, can be seen on the right. Their flag reads, 'The English Firm for Economy!' On the left is Bateman's opticians. A flag behind Bateman's sign depicting a pair of eyes reads, 'Listen! His Master's Voice – Radio and Records'.

Left: Old Town Street. Boots had two shops in the town; the Old Town Street store was open day and night. Their other shop was in George Street. The awning besides Boots reads, 'Maypole For Butter and Tea'. Next to that is the Frigidaire shop and on the other side of Boots is Henry Lawry Ltd.

Below: A tram and its driver, 1930s. The tram is standing near Derry's Clock, which can be seen in the background. Trams were a familiar sight in pre-war Plymouth and they continued to run until 1945. This was an ex-Torquay Tramways car and had a short life from 1933-36.

Above: The No. 12 route to Prince Rock, late 1930s. Also an ex-Torquay car, this one lasted until 1942. An advertisement for Hardings Furnishing Arcades can be seen on the side. The tram is in Chapel Street in Devonport, outside the premises of leather merchants G. Mounstephen & Son.

Right: A policeman directs the traffic at the junction of Basket Street and Bedford Street. Directing the busy traffic at this junction could be a hectic job at the best of times. The policeman guiding the traffic here was once known as Punch because of his red, hooked nose, though he was said to be popular with everyone.

The busy junction at Old Town Street and Bedford Street known as Spooner's Corner, *c.* 1937. Spooner's can be seen on the left of the picture announcing, 'Autumn Fashions'. This was a major site of bomb damage on 20 March 1941. On a billboard in the background can be seen the famous Guinness toucan. Balkwill's chemists can also be seen in the middle of the picture.

Telephones
Plymouth 1124 - 1125.

Registered Telegraphic Address:
Underwood, Plymouth.

UNDERWOOD'S
The Leading and Largest
TEA, GROCERY AND
PROVISION MERCHANTS
OF PLYMOUTH

Price List free on application.

SPECIAL TERMS QUOTED for LARGE CONSUMERS,
SCHOOLS, INSTITUTIONS, BOYS' & GIRLS'
CAMPS, Etc.

Carriage Paid on general orders to the value of £2 and upwards by goods rail to any station in Devon and Cornwall.

Parcels of Tea and Coffee to the value of 10/- and upwards delivered free to any address in the United Kingdom.

BEDFORD STREET, PLYMOUTH

Underwood's was the leading and largest tea and grocery suppliers in Plymouth. Situated in Bedford Street, the building was known as Trelawney House and the upstairs was said to be haunted by the late Squire Trelawney.

Westwell Street, *c.* 1940. Westwell Street linked Bedford Street to Princess Square. The city's main post office stood in this area, opposite Guildhall Square. The land was bought for the post office in 1881 and the main building was expanded in 1904. Badly bombed, the area was cleared away and part of it later became Armada Way.

Lockyer Street. The street started at Derry's Clock and was the main route to Plymouth Hoe. At its far end, before stepping onto the Hoe Promenade, there was an ornate gateway. Lockyer Street was the home of the YMCA's main hostel in the city. It was hit in the Blitz of March 1941 and several people lost their lives.

A tram passing Courtenay Street. This was one of the sixteen cars built at Milehouse by the Tramways Department. These survived until 1942, although Car 153 was damaged in the Blitz. The tram is outside Foster & Son's 'Homeopathic Chemists'. In the background can be seen the Milletts store.

Trams at Milehouse. The middle tram was an older tram from the 1920s; its livery is the original primrose yellow. These were later repainted in standard corporation colours and were a common sight around Plymouth. The trams carry advertisements for *Punch* and *The Western Independent*.

Guildhall Square. The Guildhall managed to survive the first night of the Blitz but was very badly damaged by the bombing of 21 March. It was to be demolished but the council decided to rebuild it in 1951. The work started in 1953 and the building was completed in 1959. It was reopened by Field Marshal Montgomery.

The Lido was opened on 2 October 1935 by the Lord Mayor, E.W. Rogers. Construction work was carried out by John Mowlem and Co. Ltd and Edmund Nuttall Sons and Co. A brass band played to welcome the thousands of people who turned up for the event. Not much chance of getting a swim that day!

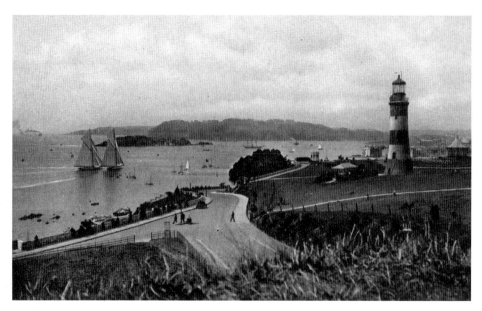

Plymouth Hoe was the scene of several bomb attacks and the Pavilion café, the pier and the bandstand were totally destroyed. The Pavilion café stood back from Drake's statue, joining Hoe Road, and was a very popular meeting place. The café was run by E. Dingle and also by Goodbody's during the 1930s.

Plymouth Pier was opened in 1870 and was one of the first structures in the city to be lit by electricity. It was destroyed by bombing, though its remains were not cleared away until 1953. Before the bombing, interest had been waning in the pier and it was steadily losing money. In its heyday, it had been a major attraction in Plymouth, with swimming contests, concerts, dancing and boat trips.

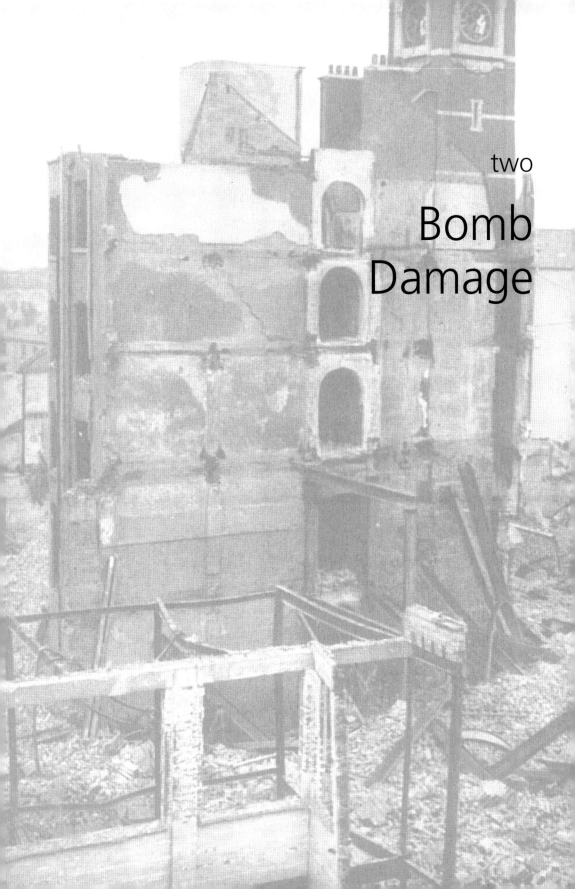

two

Bomb
Damage

Instantly recognisable, Derry's Clock still stands after the bombing of 20 March 1941. The Bank Chambers, now the Bank public house, still stand but the Royal Hotel was totally destroyed. The sign fixed to the right of Derry's Clock says, 'To the Hoe' and points towards Lockyer Street.

A view of the devastation, looking towards George Street and the Prudential Buildings. The *Western Morning News* building can be seen in the background. It survived mainly because it had only been built two years previously and was made with solid, fireproof building material. There was an underground bunker for the workers beneath the building.

Right: A policeman directs people away from the Royal Sailors' Rest in Fore Street, Devonport, while three men from the Civil Defence survey the damage. The destruction of the building, which was better known as Aggie Weston's, meant the loss of 777 beds, which had been occupied each night since the beginning of the war. The canteens and kitchens there had provided 2,000 meals every day.

Below: Boots made a vital contribution to the war effort. They manufactured 3 million lbs of saccharin, which was the equivalent of 731,000 tons of sugar, a rationed commodity. They also produced 1,500 tons of chloramine for water sterilisation in Europe, Africa and the Far East. Up to 7,000 Boots employees from all over Britain fought in the war and by 1945, 381 had been killed in battle or in air raids.

... a household name throughout the country

OVER 1300 BRANCHES IN GREAT BRITAIN

Drake Circus. On the left, in the background, there are signs among the rubble directing people to their new premises probably nearby or in Mutley, which was to become the main shopping area after the bombing of Plymouth. Before the war, Mutley had lost out to the shops of the busy city centre but after the Blitz it became the city's primary shopping centre and home to many of the businesses whose premises had been destroyed in the bombing.

Costers, a clothing and general department store in Frankfort Street, is shown here after the heavy bombing of 21 March 1941. It was well known for its school uniforms. One of the store's advertisements at the time read, 'Back to School Offer: Boys' Suits, 8 Shillings and 11d'. That would be about 44p nowadays!

Above: A policeman surveys the damage in Union Street. The badly damaged shop on the right is Weaver To Wearer, the '30 Shillings' tailors. They also had a shop where the old Criterion cinema once stood in Cornwall Street. On 27 January 1941, there was a huge explosion at Coxside when an attempt to reconnect the gas supply was unsuccessful. Three men were killed and five injured and ominous bulges were noticed in Union Street, caused by broken gas mains.

Right: The headquarters of the Plymouth Co-operative Society, which was formed in 1859 by ten tradesmen, stood on the corner of Frankfort Street and Courtney Street. The building, with its 120ft clock tower, was a major landmark in the city centre. When the building was bombed on the night of 21 March 1941, only the tower and part of the walls remained.

Searching for bodies among the rubble. During the raids of 20 and 21 March 1941, 336 civilians were killed. The further heavy bombing in April resulted in the deaths of another 590 people. On top of this, thousands were injured. Many people were reported missing and no trace of them was ever found.

Shops in wrecked Cornwall Street became known as bungalow shops because there was nothing upstairs! The first shop to be built in the new Cornwall Street after the Blitz was Ivor Dewdney's pasty shop, whose original premises were at No. 2 King Street.

Above: St Andrew's church before the bombing. The church had stood on the site for almost 900 years and it was the bells of St Andrew's that Sir Francis Drake heard on his return to Plymouth in the sixteenth century, after his voyage around the world. Although the bells survived the Blitz, there was a ban on ringing them except as a warning of invasion. This ban was lifted in 1943 and once again the bells rang out to welcome worshippers.

Right: St Andrew's church after the Blitz. The main chancel became a garden until the church was rebuilt, and flowers were planted around the pillars. St Andrew's Cross, which once stood outside, was demolished as being unsafe. St Andrew's church was reconsecrated in 1957.

George Street, seen here from George Place, was a main thoroughfare of pre-war Plymouth. Here some very official men look around in disbelief at the remains of the city. The building in the background belonged to the American Shoe Co.

Fires blazing at the junction of George Street and Bank of England Place, by Derry's Clock. The sign on the right, silhouetted by the fire behind, stood above the underground toilets. Before the war, Derry's Clock was considered to be the centre of Plymouth and all trams and buses terminated nearby. It was also a well-known meeting place – it was said that 'marriages may be made in Heaven but in Plymouth they're arranged under Derry's Clock'!

The *Western Morning News* building can be seen on the right, with the remains of the Costers store next to it. Although the building survived, its photographic department was destroyed and many photographs of pre-war Plymouth were lost forever.

The remains of George Street. Fires caused by the bombing created such unbelievable heat that thick plate-glass windows melted in pools on the pavement and gold in a jeweller's shop turned to liquid and trickled away. Cans of meat and soup exploded and, where they were packed together, they melted and fused into lumps of tin.

Perkins Corner, by Bedford Street. The overhead tram cables and tramlines on the road can be seen. A sign on the left points to an air-raid shelter. The air-raid shelters survived the bombing but were later demolished.

Tavistock Street, off Fore Street in Devonport. The Alhambra Theatre is on the right. The Alhambra opened on 19 April 1924 although the building had housed many places of entertainment before; it dated back to 1894 and was originally known as the Empire Theatre.

A gas mask rescue drill. Everyone carried gas masks with them at all times, in case of an enemy gas attack. Luckily, they were never needed. A stall in the market would inspect and repair the masks. Amazingly, gas masks were also available for horses and dogs!

The burnt-out Guildhall, with St Andrew's church in the background. Opposite the Guildhall, in Guildhall Square, stood the ornate municipal offices, which housed the lord mayor's chambers, the borough treasurer's offices and the town clerk's office as well as the Plymouth School Board. The mayor's chambers were decorated with maps, paintings and an original portrait of Sir Francis Drake. The Guildhall Square area was opened by the future King Edward VII in 1874 and destroyed in the bombing of March 1941.

George Street Baptist church, which dated from 1649, was tucked away behind the busy main shopping thoroughfare. Many other churches were destroyed in the bombing, including Courtenay Street Congregational church, the large King Street Methodist church, the Greenbank Methodist church and the Sherwell Congregational church, as well as many others around the city.

Jay's Furnishing Stores in The Octagon, Union Street. On 21 March 1941, large parts of Union Street were bombed and the entire Octagon was ringed with fire as Jay's and Service and Co's premises burnt. Further back, in The Crescent, the Westminster and Hackers Hotels were completely destroyed.

George Street. On the left is the Prudential Building, later demolished when the reconstruction of the city took place. The Prudential opened in 1903 on the corner of Frankfort Street and George Street. On the right is the shell of the George Street chapel.

Millbay station, with the old goods shed, *c.* 1941. The passenger station is on the left and in the background can be seen the Duke of Cornwall Hotel. Many railways all over Plymouth were bombed to cause maximum disruption. Others hit included those at St Budeaux, Devonport and Millbay.

A destroyed store lies in a pile of rubble on the corner of Bedford Street and George Street. The original shape of the building can be seen on the end wall of the neighbouring building. A double-decker bus is still running in the area and pedestrians make their way through the debris.

Bedford Street and Cornwall Street. The building on the left housed the Royal Liver Friendly Society on the first floor and George Oliver's underneath. Few major buildings in the city survived the Blitz. Among those that did were the Odeon cinema in Union Street, the Prudential Building, the Pannier Market and the offices of the *Western Morning News*.

The smouldering remains of No. 86 store at Millbay Docks. On the night of 23 April 1941, there were fifty-six fires throughout the city. These covered Millbay Docks, Cattedown, Victoria Wharves, Torpoint Oil Depot and many others. Water dams containing 5,000 gallons of water each were erected at nine different points around the city.

During the war, everything possible was salvaged and, if possible, reused. Here, Navy personnel are sorting items into containers marked 'Paper', 'Iron' and 'Rags'. A sign on the wall reads, 'Raw Material for War Material'. Railings were taken away from many homes and buildings around Plymouth to be used in the manufacture of armaments, although unfortunately they were never used. You can still see where the railings were cut away and never replaced on some of the older buildings around the city.

George Street. Cohen's in Bedford Street can be seen on the left, over the rubble. Plymouth had 602 alerts altogether and 59 raids in which bombs were dropped. The bombing started on 6 July 1940 and the last bombs fell on 30 April 1944.

East Street, leading to Old Town Street, with the Corn Exchange on the right. Old Town Street survived the first wave of bombing but was subsequently totally destroyed. The heaviest death tolls from enemy bombing came during the raids of March and April 1941, when the total number of civilians who lost their lives amounted to 590.

Leigham Street, on the Hoe, was heavily bombed. Before the war, these houses would have had spectacular views across the Sound to Mount Edgcumbe and Jennycliff. The Forte Posthouse now stands where these houses were situated. Leigham Street adjoined Citadel Road.

St Budeaux station was a very popular station used by sailors and dockyard workers going to work and by tourists travelling to Cornwall over the Royal Albert Bridge. It was a target for the Luftwaffe, being close to the bridge and other strategic targets such as the armaments barges and the dockyard.

Firemen hose down the *Western Morning News* offices to stop the fire in the adjacent Costers store from spreading. The building was built from newer materials and therefore withstood the blasts. After the war, New George Street was built around it.

A direct hit on a house in St Budeaux. Many gaps like this appeared in streets all over Plymouth during the bombing raids. After the war, houses were rebuilt and a modern building often appeared in the space. There is evidence of this all over Plymouth, with perhaps a 1950s bungalow in the middle of a terrace of Victorian homes.

Above: Two men help to clear away the rubble in Frankfort Street. V.B. Mills' and Wride's shops can be seen. Leicester Harmsworth House and the remains of Costers stood further to the right, out of shot.

Right: St Andrew's church, seen from Spooner's corner. The word *Resurgam*, which is now carved in stone above the main entrance of the church, was first chalked on a piece of wood and fixed to the lintel of the ruined church by Miss M.E. Smith, headmistress of the Kindergarten at Plymouth High School for Girls. *Resurgam* is Latin for 'I shall rise again'.

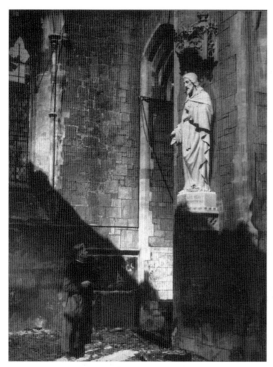

Left: Prebendary G.B. Hardy, the Rural Dean of Plymouth, surveys the damage at St Peter's church in Wyndham Square, gazing at a statue that has somehow escaped the bombing. St Peter's was much more modern than other churches in Plymouth and had a rich collection of ornaments and vestments. It was gutted by fire but its distinctive tower remained in place.

Below: A statue from St Andrew's church is rescued and placed to one side to be restored later. After the bombing, the debris was removed and the church, with its simple altar and gleaming cross, continued to welcome worshippers, while birds flew in and out from where the roof had once been. The organist, Dr Harry Moreton, led the singing in the church while the congregation gathered around what had once been the body of the church.

This photograph gives some idea of the extent of the devastation that occurred all over Plymouth. Most of the buildings in this view have been damaged and many that are still standing became victims of later bombing raids. All over the city, bomb disposal squads worked coolly and efficiently, dealing with the many unexploded bombs. At Osborne Place on the Hoe, a large bomb was being removed on a lorry when it exploded, killing five men.

Cornwall Street, with the Co-operative building visible in the background. A sign for J.C. Tozer Ltd announces that it has moved to an address in Devonport. Signs like these popped up all over the city, directing customers to businesses' new locations. Some businesses spread out all over the city and could be found trading in any available premises, including houses.

The *Western Morning News* building. The proprietors were proud of the fact that they never once stopped printing the *Western Morning News* or the *Western Evening Herald* throughout all the difficulties and dangers of the enemy attacks.

Twisted girders can be seen sticking up from the rubble at Spooner's Corner, looking across to the top of Treville Street. Fire was responsible for much of the damage to the city. Fire brigades rushed to Plymouth from other cities during the fierce attacks, but many found that their hoses wouldn't connect to the hydrants. There were so many fires that most had to be left to burn themselves out.

Two steamrollers help to clear up Fore Street in Devonport. Badly damaged in the raids of April 1941, Fore Street lay in ruins together with the adjacent areas of Marlborough Street, Tavistock Street, Catherine Street, Queen Street and High Street. Buildings such as the Belisha Hall, the Hippodrome and the Alhambra Theatre were totally destroyed.

A couple save all they can from their bombed house, including sheets and blankets. With many of the large stores which supplied the bulk of food and clothing destroyed, supplies were short and had to be rushed to the city from other parts of the country.

Phoenix Chambers in Princess Square. The devastation of Plymouth was worse than anyone could have imagined in the early days of the war. There wasn't a part of the city that escaped the attacks and scarcely a house in the area that didn't experience some form of damage, either serious or minor.

Market Avenue. During five nights of heavy raids in April 1941, there were 23 hours and 16 minutes of continuous bombing and 1,140 high-explosive bombs were dropped, together with thousands of incendiaries. Altogether, 1,500 homes were demolished or destroyed beyond repair while another 16,500 were left damaged.

Devonport station, 30 April 1941. Bricks and pieces of wood are strewn across the tracks and a house in the background has a large hole in its roof. On 14 and 15 March 1941, six bombs fell on Central Park, two of them near the Southern Railway at Devonport. Five people were killed in the bombing attacks and seven houses were demolished when six bombs fell on Royal Navy Avenue in Keyham.

George Street. Goodbody's had shops in both George Street and Bedford Street, both of which were completely destroyed. Other cafés that became victims of the Blitz included the Mikado, Williams, the Hoe Tea Pavilion and Spooner's.

The Criterion cinema in Cornwall Street was destroyed in the raids. Elsewhere in the city, there were many other picture houses lost. These included the Palladium, the Cinedrome, the Electric, the Devonport Hippodrome, the Forum in Fore Street (later repaired), the Savoy, the New Empire, the Tivoli and the Grand in Union Street. It seems amazing now that the city housed so many cinemas but this was a time when few people had televisions.

St Andrew's church and the Guildhall. Many churches were lost in the city. As well as St Andrew's, Charles church, St Saviours, St James the Less, St Peter's, All Saints, St George's, St Aubyn and St James the Great and at least ten others were destroyed.

A scene of total devastation inside the Plymouth Guildhall. On 21 March 1941, the Guildhall, St Andrew's church and the Municipal Buildings were gutted by fire after intensive bombing. Although the Guildhall was earmarked for demolition, it was eventually rebuilt and reopened in 1959.

Charles church still stands at Charles Cross roundabout as a memorial to Plymouth's war dead. The church was situated in Vennel Street until the area was obliterated by heavy bombing. The council's reconstruction committee decided to demolish the church on 15 June 1953 but it was saved and on 1 November 1958 Revd J. Allen James dedicated it as a memorial to the 1,200 civilians who lost their lives in the war. Alderman G. Wingett, the Lord Mayor, unveiled a plaque on the north wall.

Keyham station, *c.* 1941. On 29 April 1941, the GWR locomotive 4911 *Bowden Hall* was damaged beyond repair during an air raid when a bomb fell nearby. Keyham station was adjacent to Saltash Street and Admiralty Street and was opened in 1901.

A home in Pomphlett has been demolished by a direct hit. On 7 May 1941, the residents of Pomphlett had a narrow escape when a bomb destroyed three houses and damaged fifteen others. Three people were killed: Revd W. Spencer, a Navy man and a Plymouth businessman. Elsewhere in the city, bombs were dropped on Millbay, Thorn Park and Stoke but there were no casualties.

East Street ran from Cornwall Street to Old Town Street and backed on to the market. The post office can be seen in the distance, in the centre of the photograph. After the post office was destroyed, it moved to new premises at Spears Corner in Tavistock Road.

Much of Union Street lies shattered or destroyed, although the road has been cleared of debris so that traffic can still flow through. On the right is a temporary gas supply pipe running along the kerbside. The railway line ran over an arch at the top of Union Street and this and the nearby Millbay station became a target for bombing.

Fore Street in Devonport was once a very bustling area, with over a hundred businesses lining the street from Granby Barracks to the Dock Gates. These included Woolworths, Timothy White's, Lipton's and Marks & Spencer, which can be seen on the left. There were a dozen hotels and pubs and three cinemas, the Forum, the Tivoli and the Electric.

Spooner's Corner and Old Town Street. On the night of 20 March 1941, Plymouth experienced some of its heaviest bombing and the first big fire in the city was at Spooner's. Facing St Andrew's church, it had been a main feature of Plymouth for many years. The whole area became a huge furnace and despite the efforts of firemen, it was impossible to save.

Above: The Millbay Laundry, Stonehouse. The laundry had an air-raid shelter underneath in a reinforced basement. Millbay was a target not just because of the train station but also because of the nearby docks. It was the Germans' aim to disrupt life as much as possible by hampering travel and the transport of supplies.

Right: St Budeaux west box foundations. On 28 April 1941, the bombing raids centred mainly on Devonport, Bull Point, St Budeaux and Camels Head. Altogether, there were forty-two fires but the damage wasn't as extensive as in the attacks of previous nights, when large areas of the city had been destroyed.

A double-decker bus drives through devastated Plymouth. Plymouth's first alert was on 30 June 1940. The air raid lasted an hour but there were no incidents. However, the next raid on Plymouth on 6 July 1940 saw the first enemy bombs fall on the city. These were dropped shortly before noon on eight houses in Swilly Road. A man, a woman and a boy were killed and six people were injured.

A man rescues his dog from the wreckage. On 7 July 1940, Plymouth suffered its second serious attack. A German bomber flew low over the east end of the city towards Laira. The plane was so low that a man working at the gasworks opened fire on it with a shotgun. The gasworks were the target but the stick of bombs fell on South Milton Street and Home Sweet Home Terrace. A policeman and a soldier on duty in the area were killed by the blasts, together with five other people.

Bedford Street, with Cohen's visible on the left. Before the war, Bedford Street had spectacular Christmas grottos at Dingles, Yeo's, Pophams and Spooner's department stores. The whole area was very busy at that time of year and each shop had highly decorated window displays and their own Santa Claus.

Drake Circus. The building on the left housed the Liverpool Victoria insurance offices. A huge hoarding advertising Bovril covered the right-hand side of the building. Many of the buildings still standing were later torn down for redevelopment.

People go about their everyday business in Drake Circus after the main streets have been cleared of debris. The Guinness clock (top left) had 'Guinness Time' written underneath and then the company's motto, 'Guinness is good for you', in large letters.

People walk around the rubble outside David Greig's in Fore Street, Devonport, after bombing in April 1941. Two doors up is the Forum cinema. Further bombing in the Devonport area on 9 July 1941 resulted in the deaths of two policemen who were sheltering in one of the few remaining doorways in Fore Street. Seven other people were injured and eight people were trapped underneath a demolished house. They were later rescued safely.

Above: Old Town Street was severely damaged on 20 March 1941 and the Luftwaffe returned the next day to finish the job. Here, the street is being cleared of debris so it can be opened up to pedestrians and traffic. On the left is Fred Notcutt's photographers and in the background is the Guinness building.

Right: St Andrew's church, with daffodils growing in what was once the body of the church. St Andrew's was opposite the bustling Bedford Street. The bust within the church of Zachariah Mudge, who was elected as Vicar of St Andrew's in 1731, remained intact despite the heavy bombing.

The Belmont Street railway line, approaching Millbay station. The station was severely damaged by the bombing of March and April 1941 and was closed on 23 April 1941, after which the platform lines were only used for goods traffic loading.

Rebuilding work in the area of the old market and Corn Exchange. In the background can be seen Collier and Co. and Coles. Many of the old buildings of Plymouth are still standing but reconstruction has started in the background.

Old Town Street, looking towards Drake Circus. The Burton building can be seen in the middle, with Rogers and Co. on the left. An army truck drives down the road and a family, complete with gas masks, heads towards what remains of the shopping centre.

A bomb disposal unit at work. Sam Mitchell, who lived in Cothele Avenue, remembers coming out of the air-raid shelter by the Astor playing field after five bombs had exploded nearby. A warden stood above an unexploded bomb with his legs astride it while guiding everyone away with his hands. Luckily, it didn't explode.

The brave men of the Bomb Disposal Squad pose among a few of the many bombs that dropped on Plymouth but failed to go off. After France fell to Germany in June 1940, the Germans had access to aerodromes close to Britain. This allowed them to launch attacks on the South West and made Plymouth an easy target.

A wrecked German plane brought down on the outskirts of Plymouth. On 14 June 1943, an enemy plane, a Junkers 88, crashed in the garden of a house at Stoke. The house was used as a hostel for the WRNS. This was the first time that an enemy plane had actually crashed within the city. The crew were killed and were later buried at Weston Mill cemetery with full Air Force honours.

On 24 November 1941, a Polish fighter brought down a German plane over Plymouth. The four crew members successfully bailed out. One of them was wounded and had been pushed out over Plympton, while the others were taken prisoner near Bickleigh. The plane crashed near Roborough and the wreckage was spread out over two fields.

A German plane shot down on Dartmoor. On 18 August 1941, a single German bomber was shot down by the Royal Marines. It had been a wet and windy night and visibility was poor. The plane was hit by anti-aircraft fire and crashed in flames at Gawton Wood near Bere Alston. All four members of the crew were killed.

The wreckage of a German plane is examined. On 25 September 1940, there were numerous dogfights between German raiders and our own planes. Shells seemed to be bursting everywhere and it was the most spectacular daylight fight that Plymouth had seen. People came out in the street to watch and the heavy barrage made many of the raiders flee, dropping their bombs aimlessly in Plymouth Sound.

Millbay station, with two bomb craters at the east end. On 14 February 1941, ten enemy planes attacked the city. Bombs fell on Stoke and on Millbay. One fell on the roadway outside the Continental Hotel, where there had been a large dance. The hotel was badly damaged but luckily there were only a few casualties.

George Street, Devonport. In the early morning of 8 July 1940, Plymouth suffered its third serious raid. Four bombs were dropped on Devonport in the vicinity of Marlborough Street and Morice Square. A local butcher, Mr Slee, was killed when his shop took a direct hit. Three other people were seriously injured, with another seven sustaining minor injuries. Three of the bombs fell near the Royal Albert Hospital but thankfully there was little damage.

Occupants of a bombed house look to see if anything can be salvaged. Quite often, there was nothing to save and many people not only lost their homes but also their possessions and sometimes even their livelihoods.

Left: This house in Old Town Street has been blown to pieces but, amazingly, the pictures and plates have stayed, unbroken, on the walls. There were many incidents like this where fragile items survived the blasts while everything around them was destroyed.

Below: A bombed house in Mulgrave Street is cleared away to make the area safe. Mulgrave Street joined Lockyer Street at one end and Athenaeum Street, which led upwards towards the Hoe, at the other.

A house destroyed by bombing in St Budeaux. The target was probably the Brunel Bridge. On an earlier raid in the area on 28 August 1940, six bombs and several incendiaries were dropped in the countryside between St Budeaux and Crownhill. Incendiaries which threatened the woodlands were quickly dealt with by the Auxiliary Fire Service; the bombs fell away from houses and did no serious damage.

This piano keyboard is the only remnant of a bombed house. On 25 September 1940, there was a day of alerts with bombs dropped at Higher St Budeaux and near to Higher Ernesettle Farm. Luckily, there were no casualties. Another bomb was dropped on Agaton Fort, wounding two soldiers. On the same day, bombs fell on Prison Hill at Mutley and Goschen Street in Keyham, where five houses were destroyed and several others damaged.

The Maternity Ward at the City Hospital. Bombing raids took their toll on the city's hospitals and many casualties had to be cared for in adapted premises outside the city. Hardly a hospital in the city escaped damage. Those affected included the Royal Naval Hospital at Stonehouse, Greenbank, Lockyer Street and Devonport, the Royal Eye Infirmary at Mutley and the Isolation Hospital at Swilly.

A large section of Athenaeum Terrace has been ripped away by a direct hit. On the right are the offices of General Assurance. Athenaeum Terrace adjoined Millbay Road, close to The Crescent.

Above: On 30 April 1944, the Western National Bus Depot at Prince Rock received a direct hit. Three fire-watchers sheltering there were killed and sixteen people were seriously injured. There was severe damage to the depot and several of the buses were completely destroyed.

Right: It would be many years before there were enough premises to house all of the city's traders and Nissen huts sprung up all over the centre as a temporary measure. These were small, cramped and damp but served their purpose.

Above: The public air-raid shelters in King's Gardens. Many homes had their own shelters which were erected in their back gardens. These Anderson shelters were made of corrugated iron and were issued free to people earning less than £250 a year. People with higher incomes had to pay £7. They were first issued in 1939 and undoubtedly saved many lives.

Left: Many churches in Plymouth found themselves open to the skies like this one. Their walls had withstood the blasts, thanks to them being made of solid stone, but their roofs perished. Services continued to be held in some, while other congregations were moved to smaller venues.

Right: Handbells rung in the remains of St George's, Stonehouse. St George's church was located in Chapel Street in East Stonehouse. After the church was damaged by bombing, services were held at St Paul's church in Morice Square, Devonport. In 1957, the council bought St George's for £1,400 and the stonework was used to build the Lady Chapel at St Gabriel's church in Mutley.

Below: Collecting salvage from a bombed home. Regular salvage drives were organised to help the war effort. Tin, rubber, iron, steel, paper, cooking fat and even silk stockings were all collected. A popular poster during the war read, 'Salvage saves Shipping'.

Westwell Gardens were near Westwell Street but disappeared when the reconstruction of Plymouth began. They had been built over an ancient cemetery and when the gardens were cleared for building to begin, the bodies were removed under cover of darkness so as not to upset the residents of Plymouth.

A fire rages at Lloyds Bank in Bedford Street. Many of the major banks had their premises completely destroyed. These included Barclays in Princess Square, Lloyds and National Provisional in Bedford Street and the Midland in Bedford Street and Union Street.

A section of Stonehouse Bridge was severely damaged by a nearby bomb blast. The bridge was first opened in 1773; it was raised in 1828 so that Hackney carriages could provide a public service from Plymouth to Devonport.

Grocers try to put out the flames at the Mikado café in Old Town Street. Fires burned all night in Drake Circus. In the background is K Shoes, whose sign reads, 'Foot Comfort Service'. Spear's chemists was situated nearby.

The foundation stone of the Athenaeum was laid on 1 May 1818. The building was designed by John Foulston. It was severely damaged by the bombing of 21 April 1941 but remained partly standing until after the war. It was demolished in early November 1959.

Bedford Street, viewed from the Prudential Building. In the background, the road is being cleared to allow traffic to pass through. The girders at the end are from the island between Bedford Street and Basket Street. The tower of the Municipal Buildings is visible on the right and Bank Street can be seen on the left.

The view from St Andrew's church, looking in the direction of Charles church. Most of the old buildings at the top of Old Town Street were eventually pulled down to make way for the new main post office. The patch of land on the right became St Andrew's Cross roundabout.

Phoenix Chambers in Princess Square housed public offices, including the collector of income and land taxes. Princess Square was entered from Notte Street, Westwell Street, Princess Street and Lockyer Street. On 25 September 1945, the council approved the erection of temporary shops at Princess Square to house the many businesses whose premises had been lost in the Blitz.

The Forum cinema, Devonport. The Forum was severely damaged but later rebuilt and is now a bingo hall. Winston Churchill addressed a Conservative rally at the Forum in 1950 and although the rally was held five years after the end of the war, the building still looked in a sorry state.

The Mount Pleasant Hotel in Millbay Road. The heavy bombardment of Millbay station had an effect on many of the buildings around it. The Mount Pleasant Hotel was just across the road from the station and near the Duke of Cornwall Hotel, which survived the blasts.

The Crescent took a direct hit and a large part of it was destroyed; it was later rebuilt. Opposite The Crescent was a hospital burial ground which was later made into a shrubbery and garden. The area was reputed to be haunted. Many years later, the Westward television studios were built on this land.

Plymouth Argyle's ground at Home Park was another victim of a night-time raid in April 1941. The ground was thought to be a safe area, so much so that a large amount of furniture and pianos salvaged from people's homes was stored there. Unfortunately, these were all destroyed in the fires that engulfed the ground. The site was thought to be less vulnerable because it was away from the city centre.

Plymouth Pier in a sorry state after being destroyed by the many bombs that fell on Plymouth in 1941. The blitzed pier remained until the end of 1952, when the council announced that they wanted to get rid of it as soon as possible. Interest in the pier had been waning in the years prior to the war and there was no suggestion of rebuilding it as part of the reconstruction of Plymouth.

This was once the entrance to the Promenade Pier. The War Damage Commission agreed to meet the costs of £4,754 for demolition of the pier and work commenced in April 1953. The job was carried out by Eglinton Brothers of Plymouth and divers were sent below water to unbolt the many cross-members. The job was completed in September 1953.

The Hoe Slopes. During the bombing on the night of 5 July 1941, the Hoe area came under attack. Bombs were also dropped on Hartley, Crownhill, Keyham, Laira, Devonport and Beacon Park on that night. Near the Hoe, the Windsor Arms and nearby houses received direct hits. Two families were completely wiped out. The explosion was so violent that it threw one man over the treetops and his body was found 300 yards away.

A barrage balloon crew clear away the remains of the bandstand on the Hoe and sort out anything that can be salvaged for the war effort. Unfortunately, the bandstand was never rebuilt and the land where it stood was just grassed over.

The Terrace on Plymouth Hoe. On 10 July 1940, bombs dropped on Exeter Street and the Hoe district, killing five people and injuring seven. Three people were killed near the Hoe and there was damage to large residential properties at Leigham Terrace and Carlisle Avenue. Civilians experienced more terror when they were machine-gunned by the enemy planes as they ran for the shelters. Luckily, no one was hit.

The Royal Albert Bridge was a major target for the Germans and although several bombs narrowly missed the bridge itself, it remained intact. However, an artillery barge was hit, causing severe damage to the Saltash Passage area and killing several people.

Two boys survey the bomb damage at Turnchapel. On 27 November 1940, at around 7.30 p.m., an enemy aircraft dropped four flares over the Mount Batten and Turnchapel areas. Almost straightaway, one of the hangars at RAF Mount Batten was hit by a high-explosive bomb. There was another direct hit on the Admiralty Oil Fuel Depot opposite Turnchapel station. The fierce fire that followed so illuminated the sky that people on the Barbican and the Hoe could easily read their newspapers.

Winston Churchill tours the city on 2 May 1941. He spent a long time touring the devastated city and was deeply moved by what he saw. Lady Astor, the Lady Mayoress, told Churchill, 'It's all very well to cry, Winston, but you've got to do something!' His visit brought little improvement to the lives of the people living in Plymouth but it vastly improved morale.

Left: Winston Churchill in front of the Guildhall. Churchill was visibly upset as he toured the city. 'Your homes are down but your hearts are high!' he told the people of Plymouth. His visit greatly boosted morale as he toured street after street of destroyed homes and businesses.

Below: A mass grave at Efford. After the heavy bombing over the two nights of 20 and 21 March 1941, Navy ratings from HMS *Raleigh* were given the grim task of recovering the 292 bodies from the ruins. Lord Astor requested that, if he was killed during enemy action, he should have no special ceremony and be buried alongside his fellow Plymothians.

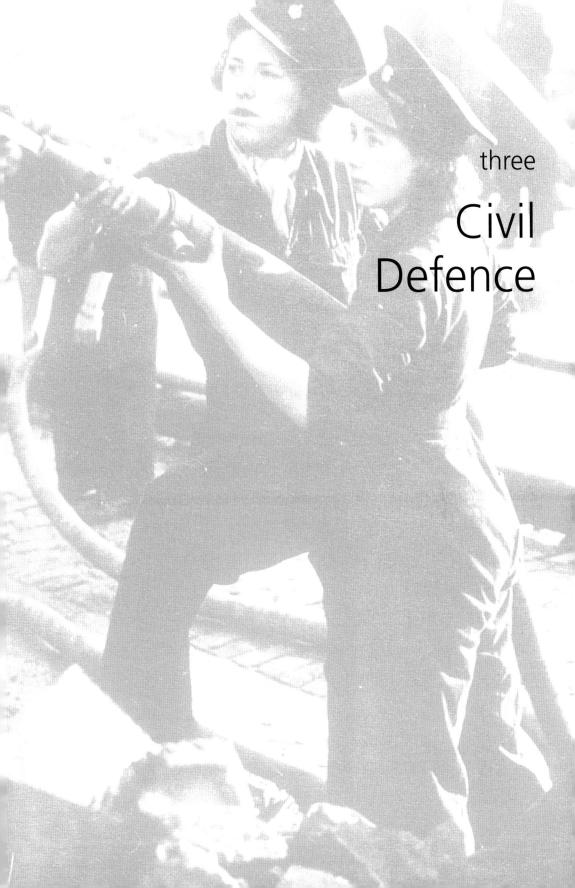

three

Civil
Defence

Left: Firefighting practice. The greater part of Plymouth burnt to the ground during the Blitz of March and April 1941 because the local brigades had inadequate resources to tackle the many fires that broke out. Many brigades from other parts of the country rushed to Plymouth's aid but then found that their equipment wasn't compatible with that of the city's. This led to devastating consequences and, frustratingly, many of the brigades had to stand idle as the city burned.

Below: A Home Guard inspection. Between April and May 1941, there were 330 full-time wardens and 1,406 part-time wardens. During just five nights in April, the casualties in the Civil Defence included forty killed and 120 injured. In 1941, an order stated that all males between the ages of sixteen and sixty, if not in the Home Guard or helping with Civil Defence, had to do forty-eight hours of fire-watching duty a month.

The Navy lends a hand with clearing up. They are seen here in Fore Street, Devonport, just about to pass the remains of the Forum cinema. The Navy, when land-based, also helped women of the WVS (Women's Voluntary Service) cook stew for the many homeless people.

Firemen and a Civil Defence worker deal with the aftermath of the previous night's bombing in George Street. Furniture is salvaged from the surrounding buildings and left waiting to be collected and reused, while a bulldozer clears away rubble in the background. The van belongs to J. Ford, who was a plumber situated in Tavistock Road.

Digging for Victory on Plymouth Hoe. With food shortages, many of Plymouth's city parks were turned into allotments. Here, the crop is potatoes. Vegetables were not rationed but were often in short supply. People who had gardens were encouraged to plant vegetables instead of flowers.

The YMCA provide tea for the troops. The British YMCA played a big part in both world wars, providing food, drink and writing materials from special YMCA huts. Their canteen was open twenty-four hours a day, supplying meals to the armed forces.

Plymouth North Road station. On 21 July 1940, the station was the target during a series of five raids. It was completely missed but bombs hit York Place and did extensive damage and also killed an elderly woman and a young boy. Another bomb hit the premises of Edmund Walker, a ball-bearing specialist, in Albany Ope and extensive damage nearby made many families homeless.

Clearing away the rubble after the bombing of Millbay station. During the night of 27 August 1940, Plymouth had its longest alert so far, with relays of German planes heading north. Bombs were dropped over a scattered area, including Millbay, Crownhill and Ford. The worst incident was when a bomb dropped on Ford House, the Public Assistance Institution. Thirteen inmates were killed and many others were injured. One young boy was saved when a nurse shielded him with her body. She was knocked unconscious but later recovered.

Above: Women salvage workers collect furniture from a bombed house to be stored away for safe keeping. Unfortunately, a lot of the saved items were later destroyed in further bombing attacks. A WVS Housewives' Section was formed in 1942. Some women with small children or other commitments didn't have time to do regular WVS work so the Housewives' Section helped by assisting the local warden and making cups of tea and helping the elderly.

Left: Lady Astor inspects the bomb damage, accompanied by a soldier. Lady Astor was born in America in 1879. She married Waldorf Astor in 1906 and they lived at No. 3 Elliot Terrace, on the Hoe. She was the MP for Sutton from 1919 to 1945. During the Second World War, Lord and Lady Astor were the Mayor and Lady Mayor of Plymouth. She died in 1964.

Two firemen survey the damage done to the Guildhall. The Auxiliary Fire Service was formed at the beginning of the war to assist the regular fire brigades. Many of the ranks were made up of women and, throughout the country, there were 32,200 women serving in the National Fire Service. Many were part-timers; men went on duty every fourth night and women every sixth night.

A search is made for any sign of life among the rubble of a destroyed building. Civil Defence workers were a liaison between the Navy, the Army, the Air Force and the civilian population. The town clerk, Colin Campbell, was controller of the ARP.

The Bomb Disposal Squad at work. On 11 January 1941, the Wolsdon Street bomb, which was one of the biggest unexploded bombs dropped on the city, was removed by the squad. It had been there since the raid of 28 December 1940. It weighed over a ton and was 9ft long, with fins another 2ft long.

The Navy helped to move salvaged furniture and belongings. On the side of the lorry is written 'We shift you quicker than a dose of Epsoms'! All salvaged furniture was carefully labelled before being stored so that it could be traced back to its owners.

Right: Women salvage workers help man the hoses. In June 1938, the Women's Voluntary Service for Air-raid Precaution was formed. To begin with, the membership was essentially middle-class and their uniforms consisted of bottle green coats and hats which the volunteers had to pay for themselves.

Below: Plymouth's women ready to extinguish any fire. Early tasks for the Women's Voluntary Service included evacuation and making medical supplies such as bandages (from old sheets), pyjamas and nursing gowns. In February 1939, with their roles ever-expanding, they became the Women's Voluntary Service for Civil Defence, though they were known more commonly as the WVS.

Above: Lady Astor looks on as women salvage workers clear the rubble. Noel Coward said of Lady Astor, 'Nobody who saw Lady Astor, as I did, when Plymouth was being bombed almost out of existence, could feel anything but profound and affectionate admiration. I remember in 1942 walking with her through the streets after a bad Blitz. She dashed here, there and everywhere, encouraging, scolding, and making little jokes. In the sitting room of one pathetic house, the roof and kitchen of which had been demolished, she ordered a pale young man to take the cigarette out of his mouth, told him he would ruin his lungs and morals with nicotine, slapped him on the back, and on we went.'

Left: Salvage workers help to demolish the ruins of a bombed building. The Women's Voluntary Service was responsible for organising salvage drives, which included the removal of railings. They also collected aluminium pots and pans, jelly moulds, kettles, paper and rubber and even artificial limbs. Much of this was never reused but the drives brought people together and raised morale.

Above: Civil Defence workers hose down a building to stop fire spreading, while others clear away bricks and rubble. The great heat generated from these fires could easily ignite adjacent premises. In August 1939, with war approaching, the Auxiliary Fire Service was issued with tin helmets, their red fire engines were repainted grey and all members were summoned to their stations.

Right: Firefighters from Exeter help to hose down a bomb-damaged building. The firefighters' resources were so stretched that many fires couldn't be reached and eventually just burnt themselves out. Firefighters from all the surrounding districts were called upon to assist with the impossible task of quelling the fires.

The Queen's Messengers Convoy were a familiar sight in the city. They were set up to feed the homeless and supply warm food and drink to people who had no electricity or water supplies. The food convoys were named after Queen Elizabeth (the Queen Mother), who donated money for the first eighteen convoys.

A group of firemen enjoy a well-deserved mug of tea delivered by the Queen's Messengers Convoy in Central Park. The side of the van reads, 'Food Flying Squad USA to Britain'. The Flying Squad was supplied by the American Committee for Air-raid Relief to Great Britain.

Women from the Salvage Service remove anything that can be saved from a bombed building. Everything was in short supply so as much as possible had to be saved. On the floor is a Kodak box with many photographs strewn around so perhaps this was the premises of one of Plymouth's many photographers.

A barrage balloon lands on the Swathmore Hotel in Elliot Street. Barrage balloons were used for low-level defence against enemy attacks. In 1938, Balloon Command was set up with the task of creating large balloons to protect major cities and installations around Britain.

The PDSA Animal Rescue Squad. Maria Dickin founded the PDSA in 1917 to provide care for animals whose owners couldn't afford their vet's bills. The PDSA had their own Animal Rescue Squad that worked alongside Civil Defence workers. Many animals were trapped and injured during the Blitz and dogs were used to find them. Many animals were awarded the Dickin Medal, which the press called the Animals' VC.

The fire brigade practicing their drill. Until the National Fire Service was reorganised in the middle of 1941, fire brigades were a local concern. This meant that the fire brigade was part of the police force and came under the command of the Chief Constable and the city council. It was completely efficient for normal fire-fighting but totally unequipped for the devastation caused by the Blitz.

four

The People

After an air raid at Oreston, this family still finds time to smile and have a cup of tea as houses lie in ruins around them. They are surrounded by the few possessions they've been able to rescue. On 28 November 1940, Oreston was bombed along with Turnchapel, Plymstock, Cattewater and the Barbican. Ten people were killed at Oreston and four houses were destroyed.

A soldier and his wife with Lady Astor. The Astors regularly visited the various shelters set up around the city for people who had lost their homes. She wrote to one friend, 'Plymouth looks like Ypres – only worse. There is so much to do that I sometimes think I'll be here forever.'

Above: Gas-mask drill for children. All children were issued with gas masks, which came in small cardboard boxes. Every day at school, they would have a gas-mask drill. Many children found the drills hard to take seriously and their masks were a source for fun and games.

Right: The Queen's Messengers at Home Park, handing out loaves of bread. The Messengers were a lifeline to the many people who found themselves without homes, food or possessions. Originally called the Food Convoys, they consisted of a few vehicles supplied with bread, basic foodstuffs, water and a field kitchen.

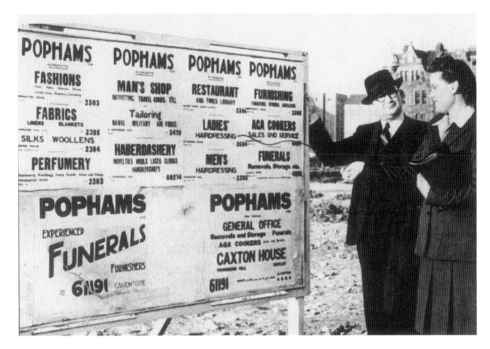

Pophams advertise their wares after being bombed out. Before the Blitz, shops such as Pophams, Dingles, Spooner's and Yeo's were all located in large adjoining buildings but after the bombing they were found operating in small shops from Mannamead to Drake Circus.

Gas masks on! In September 1942, a mustard-gas demonstration was held. The area was roped off to the public and later cleaned up with bleach. However, a day later, two boys playing in the area developed mustard blisters and had to be rushed to hospital.

Right: A National Registration Identity Card. During the Second World War, the ID card was seen as a way of protecting the nation against Nazi spies. By 1952, Winston Churchill's government had scrapped the cards because it was felt they had no use during peacetime.

Below: Children queue up to have their pets inspected by the Animal Rescue Squad. Many animals were overcome with fright during the raids. One of the boys is wearing a tin hat to protect against falling debris and rubble.

A Queen's Messengers' van draws a crowd. Many people became refugees in their own city. They had no homes to go to during the day and would spend their time in rest centres. Many would travel out into the countryside at night to get away from the bombing, sleeping in lorries, lanes or farms. In the city, the Queen's Messengers would make sure that they were well fed and had hot meals.

Armed forces proudly marching through the city. Parades boosted morale and many organisations, including the Civil Defence, the Navy, the Home Guard and the Woman's Voluntary Service, took part.

Right: Land Army girls marching past the City Museum. By 1940, agriculture had lost 30,000 men to the British Army and another 15,000 to other vital work. The severe shortage of labour prompted the government to form the Land Army. By 1944, there were over 80,000 women working on the land, doing anything from milking and general farm work to cutting down trees and working in sawmills.

Below: A man rummages through burnt books after the central library is destroyed. The library was opened on 25 October 1910. On 22 April 1941, the building and its books were severely damaged by bombing. Some books were rescued but most were destroyed in the fire. In August though, the Lord Mayor, Lord Astor, reopened the library on a temporary basis, in the museum.

Left: A young Plymouth sailor, *c.* 1941. This photograph was taken at Bayley's Studios in Plymouth. The names of 23,000 naval men and women who lost their lives in both world wars are inscribed on the Naval War Memorial on Plymouth Hoe. The memorial was unveiled in 1924 and was extended at the end of the Second World War.

Below: Chris Bailey and Barbara Hill (later Webb), *c.* 1942. Chris and Barbara both served in the WAAF in the Barrage Balloon Section. Balloon Command flew barrage balloons to frustrate enemy bombers. By the time the division had closed in 1943, it had trained over 10,000 RAF and WAAF operators.

Eric and Barbara Webb on their first wedding anniversary in 1945. Barbara had worked at Dingles in Bedford Street. Upon its destruction, she joined the WAAF Barrage Balloon Section in 1941. She was demobbed in 1946.

A trader operating from a handcart. With many buildings destroyed, businesses carried on as best as they could, either setting up in smaller premises, which sometimes included someone's front room, or in makeshift Nissen huts.

A girl with a large collection of milk bottle tops. Anything that could be salvaged was salvaged and milk bottle tops were collected for their aluminium to make Lancaster bombers. How many were needed to make one Lancaster bomber isn't known though!

MINISTRY OF FOOD
RATION BOOK
JULY 1943 ISSUE

Surname...... HUGHES

Other Names...... Charles

Address......
(as on Identity Card)

IF UNDER 18 YEARS

State date of birth (Day) .... (Month) .... (Year) ....

| NATIONAL REGISTRATION NUMBER | | | | | GENERAL |

IF FOUND RETURN TO

FOOD OFFICE

AH 722060

Rationing started in January 1940, firstly with bacon, sugar and butter. Before the war, 55 million tons of food was imported into Britain from other countries. After 1939, the government had to restrict the amount of food coming into the country because the British supply ships were being attacked by German submarines. Rationing of food lasted until July 1954.

Above: With food being rationed, huge queues formed for any kind of food that became available. Even a vague rumour could get a queue forming. Fruit wasn't rationed but was in very short supply. Exotic fruits such as bananas were rarely seen and there are stories of people not knowing what to do with them when they did get them. Some people did not know they were supposed to peel them and ate the whole lot, skin and all.

Right: Clothing was rationed from June 1941 and people were issued with booklets containing clothing coupons. People were told to 'make do and mend' so that clothing factories and their workers could instead produce munitions.

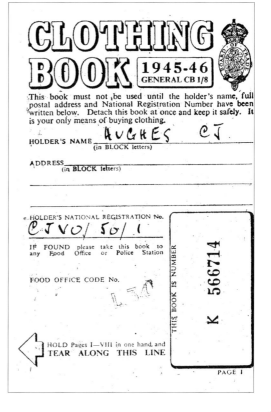

CLOTHING BOOK 1945-46

GENERAL CB 1/8

This book must not be used until the holder's name, full postal address and National Registration Number have been written below. Detach this book at once and keep it safely. It is your only means of buying clothing.

HOLDER'S NAME *HUGHES   CJ.*
(in BLOCK letters)

ADDRESS
(in BLOCK letters)

HOLDER'S NATIONAL REGISTRATION No.
CJVO/ 50/ 1

IF FOUND please take this book to any Food Office or Police Station

FOOD OFFICE CODE No.

THIS BOOK IS NUMBER

K 566714

HOLD Pages I—VIII in one hand and **TEAR ALONG THIS LINE**

PAGE I

Above: With many buildings destroyed, major shops and businesses set up in the Pannier Market. The market was equipped with new stalls which were rentable at 3d per foot per day. Housed in the market were household names such as Woolworths, Marks & Spencer, Costers and Boots. On a busy day, over 30,000 people would flock to the market.

Left: Two boys try on helmets that they've found among the blitzed debris. A favourite pastime among children was to search for souvenirs among the rubble. Helmets or other military items were highly sought after. It was a dangerous pastime, though, as many buildings were unstable and there were unexploded bombs lying around.

Above: Lady Astor waves off evacuated children.
Special trains took hundreds of children off to safe
places in the country, away from the bombs. Parcels
were packed for the children and sent on. These
included Wellington boots and warm clothing.

Right: A child's identity card. Both children and adults
had to carry ID cards. Adults carried blue cards and
children carried cream ones. If children became
separated from their parents or if their houses
were bombed, it was an ideal way for the police to
discover who was who and return the children safely
to their families.

**NATIONAL
REGISTRATION**

**IDENTITY
CARD**

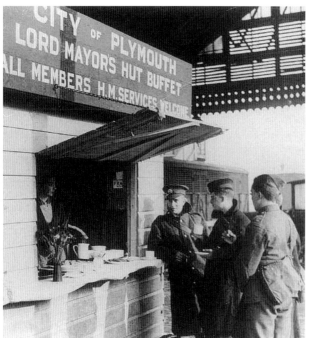

Above: Lady Astor talks to two workers. She was well known for her straight-to-the-point way of talking. She once said to Winston Churchill, 'If I was your wife I would give you poison!', to which Churchill replied, 'If I was your husband, I'd drink it!'

Left: The Lord Mayor's Hut Buffet at North Road railway station. Servicemen were welcome and could expect something warm to eat and a cup of tea. Work had started on rebuilding the station in 1938 but this had been interrupted by the war. It was 1956 before the work was restarted.

Lord Astor shakes the hand of a small boy as he is evacuated at Plymouth station. The boy has a luggage label tied to him with all of his details. In the bag in his right hand is probably a Mickey Mouse gas mask. In his left hand is all the baggage he'll need when he arrives at his new home.

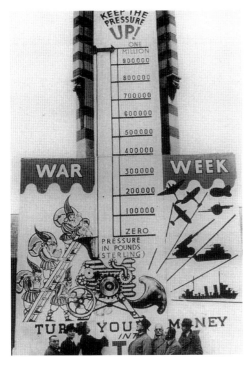

There were regular war drives to raise money to help finance the war effort. The target for this War Week was £1 million, a huge amount of money today but a colossal amount then. The slogan reads, 'Turn Your Money Into Action'.

Jim Davis, seen here aged eighteen. During the war, Jim served in the RAF as a rear gunner in Lancaster bombers. He flew thirty-three operations, firstly with 90 Squadron Bomber Command and later with No. 7 Pathfinder Squadron. Jim was later responsible for the creation of the Allied Air Forces memorial on Plymouth Hoe, which was unveiled on 3 September 1989.

Lady Astor dances with a soldier on the Hoe. Noel Coward said at the time, 'After all that devastation, on a summer evening, people were dancing on the Hoe. It made me cry – the bravery, the gallantry, the Englishness of it!'

Above: The dances on the Hoe drew people together and some people travelled from outlying areas to join in. In the background can be seen Drake's Island and to the right Mount Edgcumbe.

Right: A young girl sings with the army band at an open-air concert on the Hoe. The dances continued for many years, though when they started, the bandstand was still in position. A huge dance was held on the Hoe to celebrate VE Day on 8 May 1945.

American troops dance on the Hoe. Smeaton's Tower can be seen in the background. This photograph was probably taken during 1943 or soon after, when there was a big American presence in the city.

Lady Astor dances with a sailor. Al fresco dancing on the Hoe began in the first week of May 1941 and was a success from the beginning. The idea was first suggested by Lord Astor, the then Lord Mayor. Lady Astor was a frequent participant and among her partners was the Duke of Kent.

Right: The King and Queen at Guildhall Square on 7 May 1942. Their six-hour surprise visit was part of their three-day tour of Devon and Cornwall. On an earlier visit, on 20 March 1941, schoolchildren had lined the pavements of George Street, waving small Union Jack flags as the royal couple's car passed by on its way to Guildhall Square. Two days later, the area was blackened and destroyed after the two worst nights of the Blitz.

Below: A young soldier is reunited with his wife and child and the whole neighbourhood has turned out to welcome him home. Unfortunately, many young men didn't return from the war and those who did sometimes found their homes or families destroyed.

Above: Children celebrate Victory in Europe, waving Union Jacks around a bonfire. Up and down the country, and around the world, parties were held to celebrate VE Day. There was much merriment, along with singing and dancing. Germany surrendered on 7 May 1945 and 8 May 1945 was declared VE Day.

Left: A street party held to celebrate VJ (Victory over Japan) Day, 11 August 1945. This truly signified the end of the war and there were many parties like this all over Britain. The photograph contains very few young men as they would have all been away in the armed forces.

five

The Americans

American soldiers help with salvage work. Children were fascinated by the Americans; their only previous contact with them would have been watching Hollywood movies at one of the many cinemas around the city.

The US troops help clear up the debris. It wasn't until the Spring of 1943 that Plymouth first experienced the American Army. They had been stationed in Britain for some time before their presence was felt in the South West. A whole division, the 29th, moved from Salisbury Plain to Devon and Cornwall and set up in barracks which had previously been used by British units.

An anti-aircraft gun in the city centre. From 1943, the Americans occupied the whole of Seaton and Plumer Barracks at Crownhill and also Raglan Barracks at Devonport. Eventually they became more well known on our streets than the British troops. They were well equipped, well dressed and well mannered. They were kept under strict discipline and any misdemeanour was dealt with by their own officers or special courts.

The Americans were always there to lend a hand, in this case shifting rubble and debris. The troops constructed a 250-bed Naval Hospital at Manadon. In just two months, they had built the foundations, the camp and also equipped the hospital with everything it would need. Every section, from the nuts and bolts to the stores and equipment, came from the US. The foundations had proved a problem at first but these were made from the tons of rubble from the destroyed buildings in the city.

Practicing using a stirrup pump. There were so many American troops in Plymouth during and after 1943 that their presence swamped the few British soldiers still in the area. Both soldiers and sailors crowded the streets and shops. They had a respect for Plymouth and its people and for all that they had endured before the Americans' arrival.

Troops stationed near Saltash Passage. The Royal Albert Bridge can been seen in the background. In January 1944, the US army set up a camp at Vicarage Road in preparation for the D-Day landings. It housed 60,000 troops on their way to the Normandy landings and operated as a reception centre for returning soldiers from July 1944. It was decommissioned in September 1945.

Right: Maurice Dart lived in St Budeaux and remembers the American troops stationed at the Vicarage Road camp up the hill, above the Royal Albert Bridge. The Americans gave local children sweets and tins of cocoa and Maurice remembers being told off by his mother when he got home for pestering the soldiers!

Below: American troops outside the Odeon cinema. The Americans were probably one of the best-paid armies in the world at the time. They had plenty of money to spend and spent it lavishly. They were remembered for their generosity and friendliness. In December 1943, they threw Christmas parties for thousands of schoolchildren in Plymouth, fetching the children from the schools in their jeeps and lorries and then taking them back again after the party. The soldiers paid for the parties themselves and, as they weren't restricted by rationing, there were plenty of chocolates and sweets and every child came away clutching a toy or a doll.

The American Red Cross took over five of the large houses in Elliot Terrace, the terrace where Lord and Lady Astor lived, and turned them into a hostel for the troops. Plymouth became an important centre prior to the invasion of Europe and was visited by General Dwight Eisenhower on several occasions. His cavalcade of a large military car and armed motorcycle riders was a sight to see and became quite well known in the city.

This photograph was taken by an American serviceman stationed in Plymouth. On the left is a double-decker bus advertising 'Modern Woman' and 'E. Dingle and Co.' on the back. Prince Rock can be seen in the distance and what is now the road to Plymstock is on the right.

Gifts poured into devastated Plymouth from America. These included soft toys, food parcels, surgical dressings and ambulances. The Royal Sailors' Rest at Devonport (known as Aggie Weston's) received such large crates that they couldn't be fitted into the building.

The Americans had their naval base at Hamoaze House in Mount Batten but they also had an important naval advance base in Cattewater, where they occupied the whole frontage from Laira Bridge to Sutton Pool. After the Normandy landings, some of America's biggest warships came to Devonport Dockyard for repairs. These included the battleships *Arkansas*, *Texas* and *Nevada*.

The captured German submarine U-1023. Gradually, the American presence within Plymouth grew and it was obvious that Plymouth was to be a major starting point for the invasion of Europe. The American military activity could be seen at yards, slipways, wharfs and basins, especially in the Saltash Passage and Cattewater areas.

Jeeps and lorries outside the Salvation Army Sailors' Home, where US Navy operations were situated on the third floor. The American jeep was a familiar sight around Plymouth. The jeeps were handy vehicles with four-wheel drive. They were left-hand drive but the Americans soon got used to driving on our roads.

six

Rebuilding

Tin Pan Alley was a temporary shopping area adjacent to the market. After their premises were destroyed in the Blitz of 1941, major businesses like Marks & Spencer and Woolworths were given prime positions within the Pannier Market, while smaller businesses operated from corrugated iron stalls situated in Drake Street.

A crowd gathers around the Guildhall to listen to dignitaries and members of the armed forces as part of the VE Day celebrations. The church bells rang out over the city; previously they had been banned except to announce an enemy invasion.

Professor Patrick Abercrombie and Lord Astor. Abercrombie came to Plymouth on 19 October 1941 at the invitation of Lord Astor and the members of the Emergency Committee. He was already heavily involved with the plans for reconstructing London but stayed the weekend with the Astors at their home in Elliot Terrace on the Hoe and commented that the view of the Hoe was the only part of Plymouth that he was familiar with. It is thought that this is why the Hoe and the grand sweep of Armada Way towards North Hill proved to be the axis on which the new Plymouth was built.

Early reconstruction getting under way in Plymouth. There were many plans considered for the rebuilding of the city. Mr Hansford Worth proposed that the old streets be rebuilt with better access for traffic. Another plan was for the centre to radiate out from the Barbican. In the end, though, it was decided that Plymouth should be a more modern city with a central shopping district and recreational areas with wide roads leading to them.

The rebuilding of Union Street, which suffered major damage in the Blitz, especially around The Octagon. In December 1945, street lamps were reinstated in Union Street, Courtenay Street, King Street and Frankfort Street

The city planners: Lord Mayor Lord Astor stands beside Sir Patrick Abercrombie, with his monocle and bow tie. To the left of the picture is Mr J. Paton Watson, the City Engineer. The *Plan for Plymouth* was published on 27 April 1944. Long before the war had ended, it was realised that Plymouth couldn't be rebuilt exactly as it was before the war. The damage was too severe and the roads had been suffering from severe traffic congestion for years. The proposal put forward was to clear the lot and start again with a modern, spacious city with wide roads.

The roof of St Andrew's church is surveyed. On 22 October 1949, Princess Elizabeth laid a commemorative stone to mark the start of the rebuilding of the church. The roof was later replaced and the church restored by Frederick Etchells.

The large stretch of Royal Parade can be seen, although much of the surrounding area consists of vast cleared spaces and many of the modern buildings that we know today have yet to be built.

The steel frame of one of Plymouth's new buildings, seen from the top of New George Street. The *Western Morning News* building can be seen on the right and St Andrew's church is visible through the girders.

A double-decker bus advertising 'Gilbey's Gin' travels up Royal Parade. In 1951, Royal Parade suffered its first casualty when a Mrs Kathleen May of Fairview Avenue, Laira, died after a collision with a bus.

The new city starts to take shape. Many of the newer buildings that we know today can be seen in the background. Originally to be called Phoenix Way, Armada Way was intended to be the main boulevard of the new Plymouth.

The building in the middle of what is now Derry's Cross belonged to Levy and Sloggett, who were jewellers and pawnbrokers. The building was later cleared away and the area grassed over. St Andrew's church can be seen in the background.

It is interesting to see how many double-decker buses are travelling towards the heart of Plymouth in this photograph. The trams had been discontinued – the last one ran in September 1945 – though their tracks can still be seen in the bottom left of the picture.

Royal Parade was 150ft wide and clearing and construction of the road began on 4 August 1947. There was a plan to have a roundabout at the junction of Armada Way but this idea was rejected before building work commenced.

A quiet scene with very little traffic. On the left can be seen the newly-built Dingles building. Dingles opened on 1 September 1951 and 40,000 people visited on the first day. The familiar tower of the Guildhall can be seen on the right and St Andrew's church is in the distance.

Five years after the end of the war and Royal Parade is much as we know it today. The total cost of construction was £180,000. The street was opened in sections, with the western end being opened, by King George VI, on 29 October 1947 and the final section to St Andrew's Cross on 27 September 1948.

Other local titles published by Tempus

Plymouth

DEREK TAIT

Plymouth has seen many changes over the years and this collection of over 200 archive photographs and postcards features many images of a pre-war Plymouth now long gone. There are nostalgic glimpses of the old pier, Plymouth Hoe and the grand old theatres, where Harry Houdini and Laurel and Hardy were among the performers. This book is sure to bring back memories for all who know and love this city.

0 7524 3128 5

Steam Around Plymouth

BERNARD MILLS

This volume takes a tour along the Great Western main line from Hemerdon to the Royal Albert Bridge at Saltash, with a look at the Southern from Tamerton to Friary. The steamier aspects of Laira and Friary sheds are explored, together with the lines that served the various quays, not forgetting the branch lines that radiated from Plymouth. From Edwardian days to the BR era of the 1950s and early 1960s, over 200 photographs cover the age when steam reigned supreme around Plymouth.

0 7524 2814 4

Plymouth Argyle Football Club 1886-1986

GORDON SPARKS

Although yet to achieve its full potential as the 'sleeping giant' of Devon, Plymouth Argyle is a club that inspires great loyalty from its fans. In this book Gordon Sparks has compiled over 200 photographs and assorted memorabilia that illustrate some of the more memorable moments in the club's past. This pictorial journey will evoke many memories for those who have supported the club for a long time and provide a vivid glimpse of the past for those who are recent followers of The Pilgrims' progress.

0 7524 1185 3

Exeter Postcards

JOHN AND MARGARET FOLKES

This is an exploration of Exeter and Exonians, in the dramatic first six decades of the twentieth century, seen through over 200 archive postcards. Subjects examined include momentous events such as the arrival of the first aeroplanes ever seen by Exonians and the many crises of accidents, fires, floods and war. *Exeter Postcards* provides a fascinating visual history of the city, which will surprise some and reawaken memories for others.

0 7524 3474 8

If you are interested in purchasing other books published by Tempus, or in case you have difficulty finding any Tempus books in your local bookshop, you can also place orders directly through our website

www.tempus-publishing.com